Miss Beech unpacks some
books from a big box. She
stores the box in a corner.

"I will carry it out soon,"
she thinks.

The children all rush
in and see the box.

Seth looks at the box. "Hmmm,"
he thinks. He sits in the box.

He pretends it is a red sports car.
"Vroom, vroom. I am the winner!" shouts Seth.

Meg thinks the box is a boat. She ties her coat to a broom, for the sail.

The boat box sails in the wind.
Captain Meg stands at the helm.

The boat sails into a storm.
It is tossed about.

"Help!" shouts Meg.
"The boat is sinking."

Meg hangs onto part of the boat.
She sees some sand and swims to it.

Ben is a crab on the sand. The box is his shell. He peeps out from under it.

Next Anna gets into the box.
She flies around and then loops
the loop. The children all clap.

Miss Beech looks at the box again. "Perhaps I *shall* keep the box," she thinks.